For the Welsh children Michael, Colleen, and Emily,
and for my goddaughter, Alexis Rose Gallipoli—P. G.

To Audrey Elenor and John Edgar; thank you,
Mom and Dad—L. L.

Rabbit Ears Books is an imprint of Rabbit Ears Productions, Inc.
Published by Simon & Schuster, Inc.
1230 Avenue of the Americas
New York, New York 10020
Copyright © 1996 Rabbit Ears Productions, Inc.,
Westport, Connecticut.
All rights reserved.
Manufactured in the United States of America
10 9 8 7 6 5 4 3 2 1

Guernsey, Paul.
Noah and the ark / written by Paul Guernsey; illustrated by Lori Lohstoeter.
p.   cm.
Accompanied by an audio cassette.
Summary: A recounting of the Bible story in which Noah builds a large strong ship to save his family and two of every
kind of animal from a flood which covered the earth.
ISBN 0-689-80607-8 (hardcover)
1. Noah (Biblical figure)—Juvenile literature. 2. Noah's ark—Juvenile literature. 3. Bible stories, English—O.T. Genesis.
[1. Noah (Biblical figure) 2. Noah's ark. 3. Bible stories—O.T.]
I. Lohstoeter, Lori, ill. II. Title.
BS580.N6G78 1996 222'.1109505—dc20 92–36281 CIP AC

NOAH AND THE ARK

written by Paul Guernsey
illustrated by Lori Lohstoeter

Rabbit Ears Books

Thousands and thousands of years ago, long before the days of Moses, long before even old Abraham walked the earth, there lived a man named Noah.

Noah was a man of integrity who treated the people around him with kindness and compassion. He was a good man.

Now Noah had three sons named Shem, Ham, and Japheth. Noah and his wife taught their sons to honor all people and, above all else, to cherish the wonderful gift of life that God had given them.

But during the time of Noah, humanity grew more and more wicked. And God grieved in his heart that the people of the earth had grown so violent and cruel to one another.

You see, the people of that time thought only of themselves, and there was no room for God in their hearts. Some of the people had even forgotten about God altogether.

God was deeply saddened by the people of Noah's generation, and, though it broke his heart, God decided to destroy all that he had created.

"I will rid the earth of man," God declared, "and also of animals and reptiles and the birds of the heavens, for I regret having made them."

But God found favor with Noah, for he was the most righteous person in all the world.

And so one night God spoke to Noah: "Though it grieves my heart, I will bring a flood and send the waters over the earth to destroy every living thing.

"But fear not, Noah. You and your family will be saved, for I see that you are the most virtuous of your generation. You are a good man.

"I want you to build a boat. It is to be a big boat, an ark. The ark is to be three hundred cubits in length and made out of resinous wood."

Now Noah knew nothing about building boats. He tried to imagine the ark that God wanted him to make. *Three hundred cubits!* Noah thought to himself. *It will be longer than the tallest tree is tall.*

God said: "Make the ark fifty cubits wide and make it thirty cubits high."

Thirty cubits high! Noah thought. *It will be as high as a hill.*

God said: "Make a roof for the ark. Build three separate decks and build a window into it and put the door of the ark high up in the side. When you are finished, line the ark with pitch inside and out so that water cannot seep in."

Then God was silent.

The very next day Noah brought together his sons to tell them of the enormous task that God had commanded him to do. They set to work immediately. Noah searched for the tallest and straightest trees, for the ark would require an extraordinary amount of wood. His sons gathered woodworking tools and brought together the oxen that would haul the materials needed to make the ark. No one had ever attempted to build anything as grand as this in the history of the world.

Noah and his sons cut down the tallest trees they could find—hundreds of them—one by one. Then they fashioned the trees into boards and carted them to the site where the vessel was to be built.

They set to work with their adzes and saws and mallets to build the ark that God wanted. First the keel was laid and then the hull was built. Day after day, month after month, year after year, Noah hauled and chopped and sawed and pounded. Ever so slowly the magnificent ark began to take shape.

When the people realized what Noah was building, they mocked him. But Noah paid them no mind. While they laughed at him, he continued his work.

Noah and his sons went up and down their ladders dozens of times each day, carrying the heavy buckets filled with pitch to apply to the ark. It was difficult work, but Noah persisted. God had promised a flood, and Noah knew that God's word was true.

Noah toiled for many years and was now very old. By now his sons had taken wives of their own. But at last the ark was finished.

Noah's back was hunched over from the hard work, and his limbs ached. Noah's faith in God had been tested.

After a while Noah felt foolish because he had built a boat in a place where there was no water. *Perhaps his neighbors had been right to mock him*, he thought.

Then one day the sky grew dark.

"Noah," God said.

Noah fell to his knees and threw his hands toward the sky.

And God said: "Go aboard the ark with your wife and your sons and your sons' wives. Take two of each kind of living creature aboard the ark to save their lives with yours. One of each pair must be a male and the other a female."

Noah could not comprehend the task before him.

"In seven days' time, I will send rain upon the earth for forty days and forty nights. Remember to take with you every sort of food that is eaten by people and by animals so that neither you nor the animals will go hungry."

Noah thought to himself: *Why, I couldn't count all the different kinds of animals in seven days, let alone gather them. The animals are scattered all over the world.*

God said: "I will bring the animals to you."

The sky grew darker, and Noah sent for his sons, telling them to bring their wives. Noah's wife took her sons' wives and went into the fields to gather all the foods that were eaten by people and by animals.

Then the animals started to come, brought to the ark by God. They came from the forests and the deserts and the mountains and the grassy plains. Two by two, male and female, they came to the ark and walked up the long ramp and disappeared inside. As the animals paraded before them into the ark, Noah and his family stared in awe at the splendor and variety of God's creation.

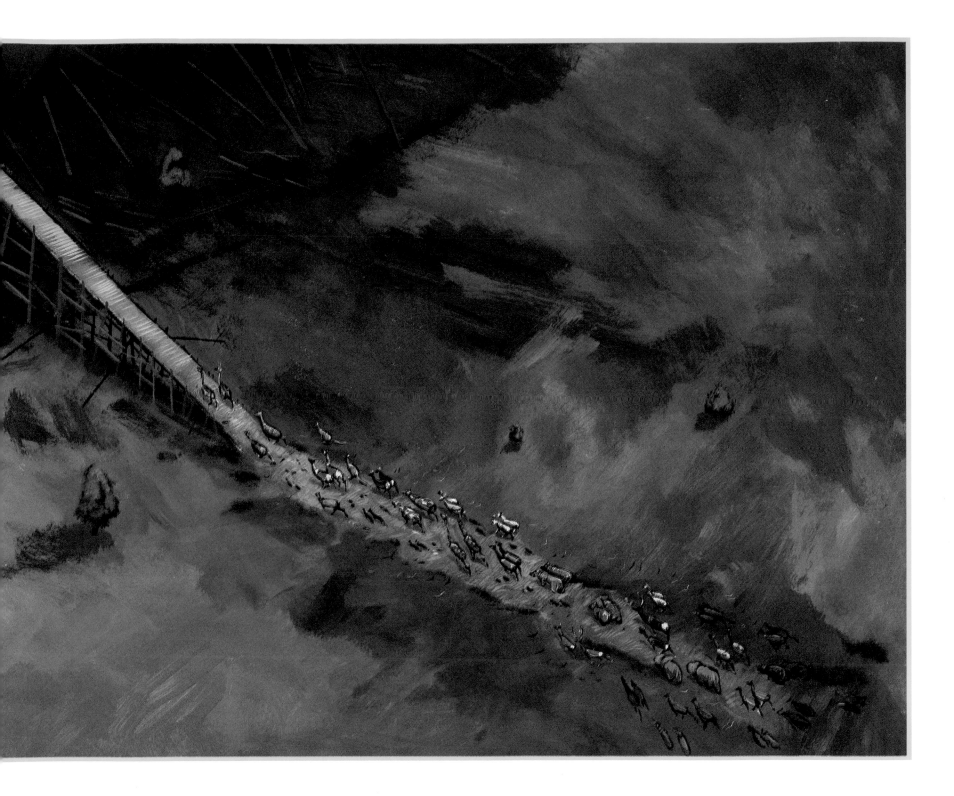

On the seventh day after God had spoken to Noah, just as the last of the animals was climbing aboard the ark, the flood began. The sky opened like a great window and the rain came down. At the same time great fountains shot up from the earth, and water burst from those springs and rose up to meet the water from the sky. As the waters swirled powerfully around them, Noah and his family climbed aboard the ark. Then God himself shut the door behind them.

It rained and it rained and it rained, and the waters rose higher and higher. Days passed, and the waters continued mounting.

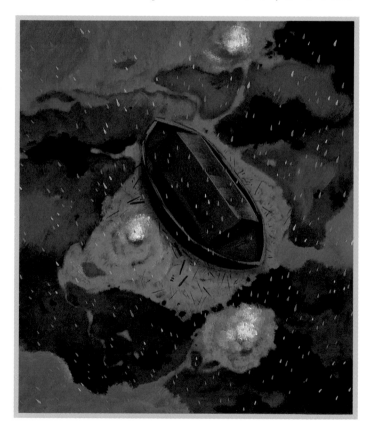

Then the beams of the ark began to creak. The boat yawed and scraped against the ground as the waters rose. The ark began to pitch and sway and finally, after many more hours, it was set afloat.

In time the great waters covered even the high hills. And still it rained.

Noah looked out the window of the ark and saw that the land where he and his family had lived was gone. There was nothing but water as far as his eyes could see. The waters covered even the highest mountaintops. And all the people and all the animals of the earth perished. All the people and all the animals—except for those in the ark.

Now there was little light in the ark. But Noah and his family were unafraid, and the animals, great and small, were at rest within the ark. The peace of the Lord was upon them.

And still it rained. The waters grew tumultuous. The waves were as big as mountains, but the great vessel glided safely across the vast expanse of water.

And it rained for forty days and forty nights, just as God had said it would.

When the rains finally ceased, the waters remained on the earth for one hundred and fifty days. All the while the ark floated without rest.

But God remembered Noah and all the beasts that were with him in the ark. He caused a wind to blow over the earth, and the waters began to recede.

Finally the ark stopped moving and rested upon the mountains of Ararat. Noah opened the window of the ark, but still he could see no land.

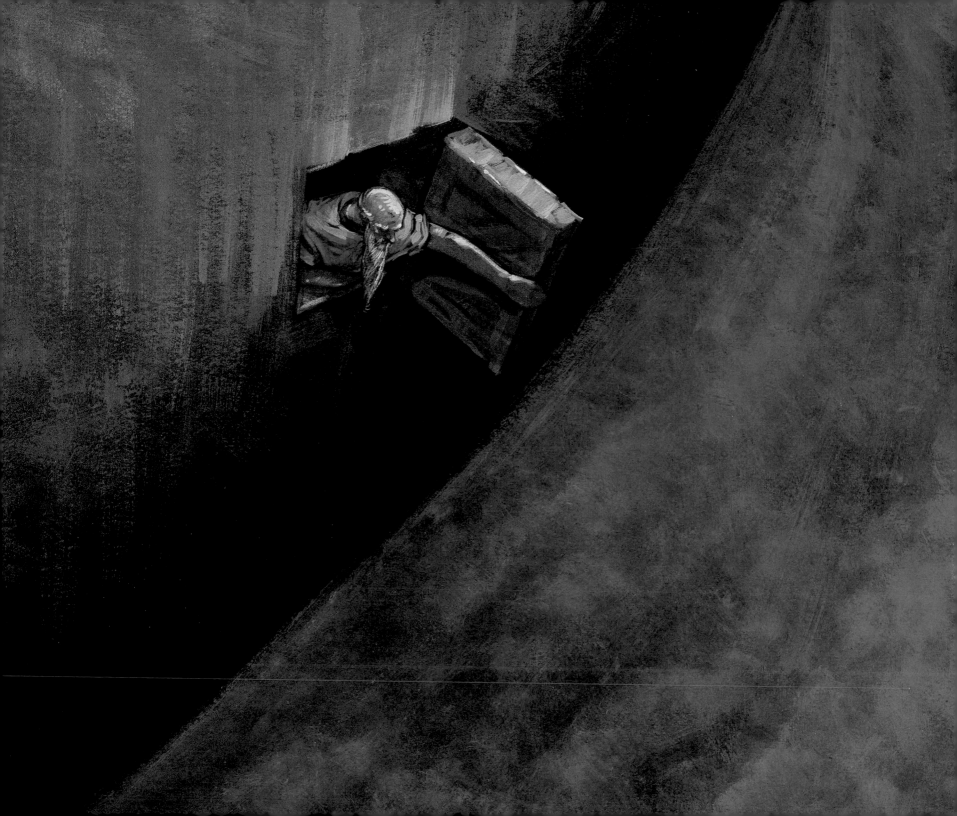

"I will send out a bird to find dry land for us," Noah said.

Now the raven was the cleverest of all the birds, so Noah sent one out of the ark. And the raven flew to and fro, but he never came back to the ark.

Noah then chose to send the dove, which was the gentlest of all God's creatures. Off she went, flying out over the water. The dove was gone a long while, and when she came back, she flew into Noah's hand and lay very still, exhausted. She had found no land where she could rest.

Seven days later Noah again sent forth the dove out of the ark.

That evening the dove returned holding the leaf of an olive tree in her beak. Seeing the olive leaf, Noah rejoiced because he knew dry land was near.

The next time Noah sent the dove out of the ark, she did not come back. Noah knew she had found a warm, dry place to build her nest.

Noah lifted back the door of the ark and looked out and saw that all the land was dry.

Then God said: "Come out of the ark, Noah, and bring all your family and bring out every living thing that is with you."

All the animals left the ark, one kind after another, and went out into the land. Each kind of animal went to its own special place in the world.

Upon leaving the ark, Noah and his sons built an altar to make an offering to God and to give him thanks.

When God saw this and smelled Noah's offering, he was pleased. During the long terrible flood, he had missed offerings such as Noah's. He looked down upon Noah and his family and looked into their hearts. And God saw Noah's goodness and patience and love.

And God said in his heart: "Never again will I curse the earth because of man."

Then God told Noah and his family what he expected from each of them now that the world was again new. "Be fruitful and multiply and fill the earth. You are all responsible for one another's lives. Your life is sacred because I have created men and women in my own image.

"I establish my covenant with you and your offspring and every living creature: Never again will I bring a flood to destroy the earth."

Then God made a rainbow appear that stretched across the sky.

"This is my bow," he said. "I will set it in the clouds, and it will be a reminder of the promise between me and all living things of earth. When I bring clouds over the earth and my bow is seen in the clouds, it will be a reminder to you, a sign of the covenant of peace between me and you and every living creature."

Noah and his family gave thanks to God for the gift of life that was bestowed upon them. God had not forsaken them.

And God spoke once again:

"While the earth remains,
seedtime and harvest,
cold and heat,
summer and winter,
day and night,
shall not cease."